T0128283

Meditations

OF THE

Overcomer

Keys for Guaranteed Success in Life

WES BRIGGS

WESTBOW
PRESS®
A DIVISION OF THOMAS NELSON
& ZONDERVAN

Copyright © 2020 Wes Briggs.

All rights reserved. No part of this book may be used or reproduced by any means,
graphic, electronic, or mechanical, including photocopying, recording, taping or by
any information storage retrieval system without the written permission of the author
except in the case of brief quotations embodied in critical articles and reviews.

This book is a work of non-fiction. Unless otherwise noted, the author
and the publisher make no explicit guarantees as to the accuracy of
the information contained in this book and in some cases, names of
people and places have been altered to protect their privacy.

WestBow Press books may be ordered through booksellers or by contacting:

WestBow Press
A Division of Thomas Nelson & Zondervan
1663 Liberty Drive
Bloomington, IN 47403
www.westbowpress.com
844-714-3454

Because of the dynamic nature of the Internet, any web addresses or links contained in
this book may have changed since publication and may no longer be valid. The views
expressed in this work are solely those of the author and do not necessarily reflect the
views of the publisher, and the publisher hereby disclaims any responsibility for them.

Any people depicted in stock imagery provided by Getty Images are
models, and such images are being used for illustrative purposes only.
Certain stock imagery © Getty Images.

Scripture taken from the King James Version of the Bible.

ISBN: 978-1-6642-0592-5 (sc)
ISBN: 978-1-6642-0593-2 (e)

Library of Congress Control Number: 2020918007

Print information available on the last page.

WestBow Press rev. date: 04/28/2021

CONTENTS

Chapter 4: Your Challenge

Chapter 5: Your Life

Chapter 6: Your Victory

INTRODUCTION

His delight is in the law of the Lord; and in His law
doth he meditate day and night.

—Psalm 1:2

Science is attempting to catch up to the truths in God's Word. Studies by
Dr. Jon Kabat-Zinn, molecular biologist researcher at the University of
Massachusetts Medical School, "found that meditation shifts a person's
brain activity from the right frontal cortex, which is more active when a
person experiences stress, to the left frontal cortex, which is more active
when a person is calm."[1] In other words, meditation literally moves our
focus from fear and anxiety to peace.

Meditating on a story or topic in God's Word by visualizing how
the spiritual truth applies to your particular situation stores the image
in your memory, allowing the Holy Spirit to change your core beliefs.

Hearing yourself say a scripture passage aloud paints a picture in
your heart when you consciously think about and focus on scriptural
subject matter.

A focus on the truths taught by the Word of God can change how
we view, think and respond to our experiences in life.

This guide is designed to take you through meditating on God's
Word to reveal areas you need to change and address to become more
Christ like. It is intended to impart faith, hope, and love to your position
as an overcomer in Christ Jesus.

---

[1] Jon Kabat-Zinn, Guided Mindful Meditation,2002, Better Listen LLC

CHAPTER 1

Your Qualification

PART 1

Your Salvation

And this is His commandment. That we should believe on the name of His Son Jesus Christ, and love one another, as He gave us commandment. (1 John 3:23)

Jesus saith unto him, I am the way, the truth, and the life: no man cometh unto the Father, but by Me. (John 14:6)

Neither is there salvation in any other: for there is none other name under heaven given among men, whereby we must be saved. (Acts 4:12)

Except a man be born of water and the Spirit, he cannot enter the kingdom of God. (John 3:5)

That if thou shalt confess with thy mouth the Lord Jesus, and shall believe in thine heart that God raised Him from the dead, thou shalt be saved. (Romans 10:9–10)

Repent, and be baptized every one of you in the name of Jesus Christ for the remission of sins and ye shall receive the gift of the Holy Spirit. (Acts 2:38)

If we confess our sins, He is faithful and just to forgive us our sins, and cleanse us from all unrighteousness. (1 John 1:9)

And ye shall seek Me and find Me, when you shall search for Me with all your heart. (Jeremiah 29:13)

I am come that they might have life, and that they might have it more abundantly. (John 10:10)

It's a choice, by an act of your will, to acknowledge your imperfections and receive by faith the Lord Jesus Christ into your life as Lord. This will change you into a realm of living like no earthly experience possible.

Your Assurance

He hath said, "I will never leave thee, nor forsake thee." (Hebrews 13:5)

That they all may be one; as Thou, Father, art in Me, and I in Thee, that they also may be one in Us: that the world may believe that Thou sent Me. (John 17:21)

I in them, and Thou in Me, that they may be made perfect in one; and that the world may know that Thou hast sent Me, and hast loved them, as Thou hast loved Me. (John 17:23)

Being confident of this very thing, that He which hath begun a good work in you will perform (finish) it until the day of Jesus Christ. (Philippians 1:6)

What comfort and assurance the Lord's Prayer is, declaring that we may become one with Him and be loved by our heavenly Father as He loves Jesus.

5

PART 3

Your Prayer

That the God of our Lord Jesus Christ, the Father of glory, may give unto you the spirit of wisdom and revelation in the knowledge of Him: The eyes of your understanding being enlightened; that ye may know what is the hope of His calling, and what is the riches of the glory of His inheritance in the saints, and what is the exceeding greatness of His power to us-ward who believe, according to the working of His mighty power, which He wrought in Christ, when He raised Him from the dead, and set Him at His own right hand in the heavenly places. (Ephesians 1:17–20)

But speaking the truth in love, may grow up into Him in all things, which is the head, even Christ. (Ephesians 4:15)

Again I say unto you, That if two of you shall agree on earth as touching anything that they shall ask, it shall be done for them of My Father which is in heaven. (Matthew 18:19)

Praying this prayer will bring you into life as an overcomer. It shows faith and your agreement with God's Word granting you wisdom and revelation of Him. You are enlightened, knowing His calling for you, the riches of His inheritance in you, and His death raising power in you.

PART 4

Your Promise from God

According to His divine power hath given us *all* things that pertain to unto life and Godliness, through the knowledge of Him that called us to glory and virtue. (2 Peter 1:3)

To whom God would make known what is the riches of the glory of this mystery among the Gentiles; which is Christ in you, the hope of glory. (Colossians 1:27)

Who is he that overcometh the world, but he that believeth that Jesus is the Son of God. (1 John 5:5)

As seeds, we grow through the watering of the Word of God. You must reckon that you have already been given all you need to walk in the overcoming life.

PART 5

Your Meditation

Engaging in Meditation

Concentrate your thoughts on what scripture says and how it can apply to you, your circumstances, and others.

- *Visualize being and doing what the scripture passage says.*
- *Speak the passage with personalization.*
- *Choose to believe this verse or subject is for you.*
- *Thank God for bringing it to fruition to, in, and through your life. This is the process of receiving the actualization of the matter.*

Blessed is the man that walketh not in the counsel of the ungodly, nor standeth in the way of sinners, nor sitteth in the seat of the scornful. But his delight is in the law of the Lord; and in His law doth he meditate day and night. And he shall be like a tree planted by the rivers of water, that bringeth forth his fruit in his season; his leaf also shall not wither; and whatsoever he doeth shall prosper. (Psalm 1:1–3)

Examples of Meditation

- *Walking in the counsel of the ungodly speaks of wrong beliefs.*
- *Standing in the way of sinners speaks of wrong behaviors.*
- *Sitting in the seat of the scornful speaks of wrong thoughts.*
- *The law of the Lord speaks of His ways, His truths, and His life.*
- *A tree speaks of being immovable.*
- *Being planted speaks of being established.*
- *Rivers speak of unlimited resources.*
- *Bringing forth fruit speaks of being productive.*
- *Your leaf not withering speaks of continual life.*
- *Whatsoever you do speaks of your choices.*
- *Prosperity speaks of overall well-being.*

The first three issues must be resolved before you will delight in the law of the Lord. Then your meditation blessings will be effective.

CHAPTER 2

Your Identity

PART 6

Your Location

You are where you are based on what's in your heart.

> And the Lord called unto Adam, and said unto him, where art thou? (Genesis 3:9)

Where are you?
Your condition is not your position in Christ. The fact is you may be going through some things, but the truth is that "you are seated with Christ Jesus in heavenly places" (Ephesians 2:6).

> Beloved, think it not strange concerning the fiery trial which is to try you, as though some strange thing happened unto you. (1 Peter 4:12)

Trials introduce people to themselves, exposing core beliefs.

> As you have therefore received Christ Jesus the Lord, so walk ye in Him: rooted and built up in Him, and be established in the faith, as ye have been taught, abounding therein with thanksgiving. (Colossians 2:6–7)

Thankfulness in and through a trial demonstrates our faith in God to bring us out of the trial with a more Christ like character than before the trial.

PART 7

Your Position

You are who you are in your heart.

> For as he thinketh in his heart, so is he. (Proverbs 23:7)

Who are you?
What you are thinking is based on current or past experiences, whether conscious or subconscious. It is derived by your perception (image) of the event.
Pictures are the language of our hearts.
Negative images produce self-destructive thoughts, such as I'm not so bad or I'm not good enough according to you, others, or God's standards. These self-destructive thoughts produce negative energy patterns in our minds and bodies, causing false beliefs and unhealthy bodies.

> Finally, brethren, whatsoever things are true, whatsoever things are honest, whatsoever things are just, whatsoever things are pure, whatsoever things are lovely, whatsoever things are of good report; if there be any virtue, and if there be any praise, think on these things. (Philippians 4:8)

Changing your thinking will change your beliefs. Always consider God's perspective concerning the matter.

PART 8

Your Words

What you say is based on what's in your heart.

> But those things which proceed out of the mouth come forth from the heart. (Matthew 15:18)

> For out of the abundance of the heart the mouth speaketh. (Matthew12:34)

What is coming out of your mouth?

> Death and life are in the power of the tongue: and they that love it shall eat the fruit thereof. (Proverbs 18:21)

> Whoso keepeth his mouth and his tongue keepeth his soul from troubles. (Proverbs 21:23)

> My mouth shall speak of wisdom; and the meditation of my heart shall be of understanding. (Psalm 49:3)

Speak God's Word—truth, not facts—in faith over your life and your situation, and watch God change you and your circumstances.

PART 9

Your Faith

You speak what you believe.

> With the heart man believeth unto righteousness, and
> with the mouth confession is made unto salvation.
> (Romans 10:10)

What are you believing?
The Holy Spirit gives revelation for you to choose what you
believe.

> Howbeit when He, the Spirit of truth, is come, He
> will guide you into all truth: for He shall not speak of
> Himself; but whatsoever He shall hear, that shall He
> speak: and He will shew you things to come. (John
> 16:13)

Correction of erroneous beliefs requires acknowledgment and
taking responsibility. Hearing yourself speak truth incites faith for
change.

PART 10

Your Actions

You will always do what you believe in your heart.

> I the Lord search the heart; I try the reins, even to give every man according to his ways, and according to the fruit of his doings. (Jeremiah 7:10)

What is your behavior?

> I will instruct thee and teach thee in the way which thou shalt go: I will guide thee with Mine eye. Be ye not as the horse or as the mule, which have no understanding: whose mouth must be held in with bit and bridle, lest they come near unto thee. (Psalm 32:8–9)

Our behaviors are linked to our thoughts and influenced by knowledge stored in our minds. Our natural tendency is to seek pleasure and avoid pain. We tend to act the way we feel. Are our feelings productive or harmful?

The will and ability to perform this challenge from our Lord comes only by sincere yieldedness to the Holy Spirit's empowerment.

> Keep thy heart with all diligence; for out of it are the issues of life. (Proverbs 4:23)

PART 11

Your Priorities

Your priorities are determined by what's in your heart.
Where are your priorities? That which you want or is easiest.

Therefore take no thought, saying, what shall we eat?
Or, what shall we drink? Or, Wherewithal shall we be
clothed? For all these things do the Gentiles seek: for
your heavenly Father knoweth that ye have need of
all these things. But seek ye first the kingdom of God,
and His righteousness; and all these things shall be
added to you. (Matthew 6:31–33)

Trust in the Lord with *all* your heart, and lean not unto
your own understanding, in *all* thy ways acknowledge
Him and He will direct thy paths. (Proverbs 3:5–6)

*Prioritizing your focus on the Lord first is necessary to receive
God's provision.*

CHAPTER 3

Your Objective

PART 12

Your Goal

Wherefore by their fruits ye shall know them. (Matthew 7:20)

The fruit of your life represents the condition of your heart.

The fruit of the Spirit is love, joy, peace, longsuffering, gentleness, goodness, faith, meekness, temperance. (Galatians 5:22–23)

Our natural tendency is to respond according to logic and emotions.

Choose to "love one another, as I have loved you" (John 15:12).

Invite the Holy Spirit to fill you daily with Himself.

PART 13

Your Love

And now abideth these three faith, hope, love; but the greatest of these is love. (1 Corinthians 13:13)

This is My commandment, That ye love one another, as I have loved you. (John 15:12)

Love suffereth long, and is kind; love envieth not; love vaunteth not itself, is not puffed up, doth not behave itself unseemly, seeketh not her own, is not easily provoked, thinketh no evil, rejoiceth not in iniquity, but rejoiceth in the truth, beareth all things, believeth all things, hopeth all things, endureth all things. Love never faileth. (1 Corinthians 13:4–8)

There is no fear in love; but perfect love casteth out fear: because fear hath torment. He that feareth is not made perfect in love. (1 John 4:18)

But whoso keepeth His word, in him verily is the love of God perfected; hereby know we that are in Him. (1 John 2:5)

For if our heart condemn us, God is greater than our heart, and knoweth all things. Beloved, if our heart

condemn us not, then have we confidence toward
God. (1 John 3:20–21)

For God hath not given us the spirit of fear, but of
power, and of love, and a sound mind. (II Timothy 1:7)

*Contrary to perfect love is fear, which manifests as wrong
beliefs and harmful actions. Fear reacts to pain and causes all
other negative reactions that inhibit our spiritual growth.*

*Identify areas for improvement by yielding your heart to the
Lord for changing into His image.*

PART 14

Your Joy

Thou wilt shew me the path of life: in Thy presence is fullness of joy; at Thy right hand are pleasures for evermore. (Psalm 16:11)

For the joy of the Lord is your strength. (Nehemiah 8:10)

If ye keep My commandments, ye shall abide in My love; even as I have kept My Father's commandments, and abide in His love. These things have I spoken to you, that My joy might remain in you, and that your joy might be full. (John 15:10–11)

Praise brings His presence, and His presence brings joy.

PART 15

Your Peace

Thou wilt keep him in perfect peace, whose mind is stayed on Thee: because he trusteth in Thee. (Isaiah 26:3)

Grace and peace be multiplied unto you through the knowledge of God, and of Jesus our Lord. (2 Peter 1:2)

Let the peace of God rule in your hearts, to the which also ye are called in one body; and be ye thankful. (Colossians 3:15)

Great peace have they which love Thy law: and nothing shall offend them. (Psalm 119:165)

And the work of righteousness shall be peace; and the effect of righteousness, quietness and assurance forever. (Isaiah 32:17)

Peace is not dependent upon circumstances.
As we allow God's love to and through us, we will have peace. When we make a commitment, with God's help, to allow His peace to rule in our hearts, we will find stress diminishing in our lives.

PART 16

Your Long-Suffering and Patience

But Thou, O Lord, art a God full of compassion, and gracious, longsuffering, and plenteous in mercy and truth. (Psalm 86:15)

For ye have need of patience, that after ye have done the will of God, ye might receive the promise. (Hebrews 10:36)

Knowing this, that the trying of your faith worketh patience. But let patience have her perfect work that ye may be perfect, and entire, wanting nothing. (James 1:3–4)

Strengthened with all might, according to His glorious power, unto all patience and longsuffering with joyfulness. (Colossians 1:11)

Now the God of patience and consolation grant you to be likeminded one toward another according to Christ Jesus. (Romans 15:5)

Seeking God's wisdom, understanding and insight enables us to see from God's perspective about His plan and purpose. We can then have patience, through God, with ourselves and others.

PART 17

Your Gentleness-Kindness

For His merciful kindness is great toward us: and the truth of the Lord endureth forever. Praise ye the Lord. (Psalm 117:2)

For the mountains shall depart, and the hills be removed; but My kindness shall not depart from thee, neither shall the covenant of My peace be removed, saith the Lord that hath mercy on thee. (Isaiah 54:10)

It is of the Lord's mercies that we are not consumed, because His compassions fail not. They are new every morning: great is Thy faithfulness. (Lamentations 3:22–23)

Reflecting on how God has not dealt with us according to our sins, we can choose to be gentle and kind to others.

PART 18

Your Goodness

Oh how great is Thy goodness, which thou hast laid up for them that fear Thee; which Thou hast wrought for them that trust in Thee before the sons of men. Thou shalt hide them in the secret of Thy presence from the pride of man: Thou shalt keep them secretly in a pavilion from the strife of tongues. Blessed be the Lord: for He hath showed me His marvelous kindness in a strong city. (Psalm 31:19–21)

Oh that men would praise the Lord for his goodness, and for His wonderful works to the children of men! (Psalm 107:15)

O give thanks unto the Lord, for He is good: for His mercy endureth forever. (Psalm 107:1)

Do good to them that hate you ...That you may be the children of your Father which is in heaven. (Matthew 5:44, 45)

Choosing to be good requires looking from God's perspective at the individual who really needs insight and love.

PART 19

Your Faithful Faith

The Lord is faithful, who shall stablish you, and keep you from evil.
(2 Thessalonians 3:3)

The Lord is my strength and my shield; my heart trusted in Him, and I am helped: therefore my heart greatly rejoiceth; and with my song will I praise Him. (Psalm 28:7)

So faith cometh by hearing, and hearing by the word of God. (Romans 10:17)

Looking unto Jesus the author and finisher of our faith; who for the joy that was set before Him endured the cross, despising the shame, and is set down at the right hand of the throne of God. (Hebrews 12:2)

Now faith is the substance of things hoped for, the evidence of things not seen. (Hebrews 11:1)

And this is the confidence that we have in Him that, if we ask anything according to His will, He heareth us: And if we know He hear us, whatsoever we ask, we know we have the petitions that we desired of Him. (1 John 5:14–15)

For in Jesus Christ neither circumcision availeth anything, nor uncircumcision; but faith worketh by love. (Galatians 5:6)

"and this is the victory that overcometh the world, even our faith."
(I John 5:4)

True faith produces corresponding works. You know where your faith is by your works.

PART 20

Your Humility

Take My yoke upon you, and learn of Me; for I am meek and lowly in heart: and ye shall find rest for your souls. (Matthew 11:29)

Only by pride cometh contention: but with the well advised is wisdom. (Proverbs 13:10)

When pride cometh, then cometh shame: but with the lowly is wisdom. (Proverbs 11:2)

We can choose humility or be forced to it. The Lord will speak to us. If we don't acknowledge Him, He will speak to us through someone. If we still will not heed, then a circumstance will arise to strongly encourage us to consider humbling ourselves before Him. If we choose to be stiff-necked, then discipline follows, which can be very unpleasant.

PART 21

Your Temperance and Self Control

There is therefore now no condemnation to them which are in Christ Jesus, who walk not after the flesh, but after the Spirit. (Romans 8:1)

For if we live after the flesh, ye shall die: but if ye through the Spirit do mortify the deeds of the body, ye shall live. (Romans 8:13)

And they that are Christ's have crucified the flesh with the affections and lust. (Galatians 5:23)

Let all bitterness and wrath, and anger, and clamour, and evil speaking, be put away from you, with all malice. (Ephesians 4:31)

The discretion of a man deferreth his anger; and it is his glory to pass over a transgression. (Proverbs 19:11)

Practice self-control until it becomes a habit. According to neuroscience, "it takes 21 days to form a habit and 63 days for it to become part of your subconscious as an automatic response."[2]

---

[2] Caroline Leaf, *Think Learn Succeed* (Dallas: Baker, 2018), 233.

CHAPTER 4

Your Challenge

PART 22

Your Acknowledgment

Have mercy upon me, O God, according to Thy lovingkindness: according unto the multitude of Thy tender mercies blot out my transgressions. Wash me thoroughly from mine iniquity, and cleanse me from my sin. For I acknowledge my transgressions: and my sin is ever before me. (Psalm 51:1-3)

Create in me a clean heart, O God; and renew a right spirit within me. (Psalms 51:10)

Humble yourself in the sight of the Lord, and He shall lift you up. (James 4:10)

But if we walk in the light, as He is in the light, we have fellowship one with another, and the blood of Jesus Christ His Son cleanseth us from all sin. (1 John 1:7)

By mercy and truth iniquity is purged. (Proverbs 16:6)

The goodness of God leadeth thee to repentance. (Romans 2:4)

It's His conviction in our hearts that changes our minds, thus changing our attitudes.

PART 23

Your Confession

Let the words of my mouth and the meditation of my heart, be acceptable in Thy sight, O Lord, my strength, and my Redeemer. (Psalm 19:14)

The grace of God allows us to see the areas of our lives that we need to bring before Him for change.
Erroneous beliefs prevent us from receiving God's promises.

PART 24

Your Sacrifice

Then Jesus said to His disciples, if any man will come after Me, let him deny himself, and take up his cross, and follow Me. (Matthew 16:24)

I beseech you therefore, brethren, by the mercies of God, that ye present your bodies a living sacrifice, holy, acceptable unto God, which is your reasonable service. And be not conformed to this world: but be ye transformed by the renewing of your mind that ye may prove what is that good, and acceptable, and perfect will of God. (Romans 12:1–2)

For the weapons of our warfare are not carnal, but mighty through God to the pulling down of strong holds; Casting down imaginations, and every high thing that exalteth itself against the knowledge of God, and bringing into captivity every thought to the obedience of Christ. (2 Corinthians 10:4–5)

Submit yourself therefore to God. Resist the devil, and he will flee from you. (James 4:7)

We must cooperate with God for the changes to be effectual in our lives.

PART 25

Your Freedom

And ye shall know the truth, and the truth shall make you free. (John 8:32)

Finally, my brethren, be strong in the Lord, and the power of His might. (Ephesians 6:10)

Be sober, be vigilant; because your adversary the devil, as a roaring lion, walketh about, seeking whom he may devour: Whom resist stedfast in the faith, knowing that the same afflictions are accomplished in your brethren that are in the world. But the God of all grace, Who hath called us unto His eternal glory by Christ Jesus, after that ye have suffered a while, make you perfect, stablish, strengthen, settle you. (1 Peter 5:8–10)

For we wrestle not against flesh and blood, but against principalities, against powers, against the rulers of the darkness of this world, against spiritual wickedness in high places. Wherefore take unto you the whole armour of God that ye may be able to withstand in the evil day, and having done all, to stand. (Ephesians 6:12–13)

Being filled with the fruits of righteousness, which are by Jesus Christ, unto the glory and praise of God. (Philippians 1:11)

Warfare is inevitable. It verifies your commitment to stand. It makes you stronger. Take the authority given you in Jesus's name, stand, and command evil to leave. Bring every thought into the obedience of Christ.

Stand fast therefore in the liberty wherewith Christ has made us free, and be not entangled again with the yoke of bondage. (Galatians 5:1)

CHAPTER 5

Your Life

PART 26

Your Vision

But we all, with open face beholding as in a glass the glory of the Lord, are changed into the same image from glory to glory, even as by the Spirit of the Lord. (2 Corinthians 3:18)

Thy word is a lamp unto my feet, and a light unto my path. (Psalm 119:105)

And He brought him forth abroad, and said, Look now toward heaven, and tell the stars, if thou be able to number them: and He said unto him, so shall thy seed be. And he believed in the Lord; and He counted it to him for righteousness. (Genesis 15:5–6)

Where there is no vision, the people perish. (Proverbs 29:18)

Correct beliefs enlarge your vision. Images create thoughts, produce actions, result in habits, establish character, and determine destiny. Believe, embrace, and see yourself in the vision.

PART 27

Your Declarations

I can do all things through Christ which strengtheneth me. (Philippians 4:13)

Because greater is He that is in you, than he that is in the world. (1 John 4:4)

Bless the Lord, O my soul: and all that is within me, bless His holy name. Bless the Lord, O my soul, and forget not all His benefits: Who forgiveth all thine iniquities, Who healeth all thy diseases; Who redeemeth thy life from destruction; Who crowneth thee with lovingkindness and tender mercies; Who satisfieth thy mouth with good things; so that thy youth is renewed like the eagle's. (Psalm 103:1–5)

Thou shalt also decree a thing, and it shall be established unto thee: and the light shall shine upon thy ways. (Job 22:28)

For verily I say unto you, That whosoever shall say unto this mountain, Be thou removed, and be thou cast into the sea; and shall not doubt in his heart, but shall believe that those things which he saith shall come to pass; he shall have whatsoever he saith. (Mark 11:23)

That the communication of thy faith may become effectual by the acknowledging of every good thing which is in you in Christ Jesus. (Philemon 1:6)

A key of the kingdom is to speak His promises to yourself often daily.

PART 28

Your Growth

Every branch that beareth fruit, He purgeth it, that it may bring forth more fruit. (John 15:2)

I am the vine, ye are the branches: He that abideth in Me, and I in him, the same bringeth forth much fruit, for without Me ye can do nothing. (John 15:5)

If ye abide in Me, and My words abide in you, ye shall ask what ye will, and it shall be done unto you. Herein is My Father glorified, that ye bear much fruit; so shall ye be My disciples. (John 15:7–8)

Wherein ye greatly rejoice, though now for a season, if need be, ye are in heaviness through manifold temptations: That the trial of your faith, being much more precious than gold that perisheth, though it be tried with fire, might be found unto praise and honor and glory at the appearing of Jesus Christ. (1 Peter 1:6–7)

Nay, in all these things we are more than conquerors through Him that loved us. (Romans 8:37)

You are pruned to grow more.
Speaking God's Word in faith releases God's blessings to you.

PART 29

Your Strength

Fear thou not; for I am with thee: be not dismayed; for I am thy God: I will strengthen thee; yea, I will help thee; yea, I will uphold thee with the right hand of My righteousness. (Isaiah 41:10)

And He said unto me, My grace is sufficient for thee: for My strength is made perfect in weakness. (II Corinthians 12:9)

Finally, my brethren, be strong in the Lord, and the power of His might. (Ephesians 6:10)

These words are declared commandments of God: Do not fear. His presence is with you. He is your possession. His strength is in you. His assistance is for you. His empowerment is through you. Trust in the Lord's strength. He will not fail you.

PART 30

Your Rest

There remaineth therefore a rest to the people of God. For he that is entered into His rest, he also hath ceased from his own works, as God did from His. (Hebrews 4:9–10)

Jesus answered and said unto them, This is the work of God, that ye believe on Him whom He hath sent. (John 6:29)

Being confident of this very thing, that He which hath begun a good work in you will perform it until the day of Jesus Christ. (Philippians 1:6)

Casting all your care upon Him; for He careth for you. (1 Peter 5:7)

Come unto Me, all ye that labor and are heavy laden, and I will give you rest. (Matthew 11:28)

Rest without stress.

PART 31

Your Destiny

Fear not, little flock; for it is your Father's good pleasure to give you the kingdom. (Luke 12:32)

Behold, the kingdom of God is within you. (Luke 17:21)

But rather seek ye kingdom of God; and all these things shall be added unto you. (Luke 12:31)

For the upright shall dwell in the land, and the perfect shall remain in it. (Proverbs 2:21)

For the kingdom is not meat and drink; but righteousness, and peace, and joy in the Holy Ghost. (Romans 14:17)

To experience kingdom living, choose to move into it.

PART 32

Your Inheritance

Looking unto Jesus, the author and finisher of our faith; Who for the joy that was set before Him endured the cross, despising the shame, and is set down at the right hand of the throne of God. (Hebrews 12:2)

In Whom we have redemption through His blood, the forgiveness of sins, according to the riches of His grace. (Ephesians 1:7)

To him that overcometh will I grant to sit with me in My throne, even as I also overcame, and am set down with My Father in His throne. (Revelations 3:21)

And hath raised us up together, and made us sit together in heavenly places in Christ Jesus. (Ephesians 2:6)

Acknowledge and accept your position, provided by His grace.

CHAPTER 6

Your Victory

PART 33

Your Testimony

And they overcame him by the blood of the Lamb, and by the word of their testimony; and they loved not their lives unto the death. (Revelation 12:11)

But thanks be to God, which giveth us the victory through our Lord Jesus Christ. (1 Corinthians 15:57)

The law of the Lord is perfect, converting the soul: the testimony of the Lord is sure, making wise the simple. (Psalm 19:7)

And all things are of God, Who hath reconciled us to Himself by Jesus Christ, and have given to us the ministry of reconciliation. (2 Corinthians 5:18)

To wit, that God was in Christ, reconciling the world unto Himself, not imputing their trespasses unto them; and hath committed unto us the word of reconciliation. (2 Corinthians 5:19)

Your personal testimony is powerful. It cannot be argued nor refuted.

PART 34

Your Anointing

The Spirit of the Lord God is upon me; because the Lord hath anointed me to preach good tidings unto the meek; He hath sent me to bind up the brokenhearted, to proclaim liberty to the captives, and the opening of the prison to them that are bound; To proclaim the acceptable year of the Lord, and the day of vengeance of our God; to comfort all that mourn; To appoint them that mourn in Zion, to give unto them beauty for ashes, the oil of joy for mourning, the garment of praise for the spirit of heaviness; that they might be called trees of righteousness, the planting of the Lord, that He might be glorified. (Isaiah 61:1–3)

But the anointing which ye have received of Him abideth in you. (1 John 2:27)

Blessed be God, even the Father of our Lord Jesus Christ, the Father of mercies, and the God of all comfort; Who comforteth us in all our tribulation, that we may be able to comfort them which are in any trouble, by the comfort wherewith we ourselves are comforted of God. (2 Corinthians 1:3–4)

Herein is our love made perfect, that we may have boldness in the day of judgment: because as He is, so are we in this world. (1 John 4:17)

The anointing

- *supernaturally enables you to perform your ministry,*
- *brings hope and good news to the afflicted,*
- *heals the brokenhearted,*
- *proclaims liberty to the captives,*
- *sets prisoners free,*
- *proclaims the acceptable year of the Lord,*
- *announces the day of God's vengeance and justice,*
- *comforts all who mourn,*
- *furnishes beauty for those who have lost it,*
- *provides happiness and a glad heart,*
- *supplies an opportunity to praise God's name, and*
- *glorifies the Lord.*

PART 35

Your Commitment

Though He slay me, yet shall I trust in Him. (Job 13:25)

But He knoweth the way that I take: when He hath tried me, I shall come forth as gold. (Job 23:10)

Commit thy works unto the Lord, and thy thoughts shall be established. (Proverbs 16:3)

Because thou hast made the Lord, which is my refuge, even the most High, thy habitation;
There shall no evil befall thee, neither any plague come nigh my dwelling...
Because he hath set his love upon Me, therefore I will deliver him: I will set him on high, because he hath known My name.
He shall call on Me, and I will be with him in trouble; I will deliver him. With long life will I satisfy him, and show him My salvation.
Psalm 91:9-10, 14-16)

Surely goodness and mercy shall follow me all the days of my life: and I will dwell in the house of the Lord forever. (Psalm 23:6)

Whereby are given to us exceeding great and precious promises: that by these ye might be partakers of the divine nature, having escaped the corruption that is in the world through lust. And beside this, giving *all diligence*, add to your faith virtue; and to virtue knowledge; and to your knowledge temperance; and to your temperance patience; and to patience godliness; and to godliness brotherly kindness; and to brotherly kindness love. For if these things be in you, and abound, they make you that ye shall neither be barren nor unfruitful in the knowledge of our Lord Jesus Christ. But he that lacketh these things is blind, and cannot see afar off, and hath forgotten that he was purged from his old sins. Wherefore the rather, brethren, give diligence to make your calling and election sure: for if ye do these things, ye shall never fall: For so an entrance shall be ministered unto you abundantly into the everlasting kingdom of our Lord and Saviour Jesus Christ. (2 Peter 1:4–8)

Spend time meditating on God's Word. Apply His promises to your life. It will change you from the inside out as a partaker in His divine nature.

PART 36

Your Choice

I have set before you life and death, blessing and cursing: therefore choose life, that both thou and thy seed may live. (Deuteronomy 30:19)

While the earth remaineth, seedtime and harvest, and cold and heat, summer and winter, and day and night shall not cease. (Genesis 8:22)

Let this mind be in you, which was also in Christ Jesus: And being found in fashion as a man, He humbled Himself, and became obedient unto death, even the death of the cross.
Wherefore God hath highly exalted Him, and given Him a name which is above every name. (Philippians 2:5...8, 9)

Then Isaac sowed in that land, and received in the same year an hundredfold: and the Lord blessed him. (Genesis 26:12)

Begin Today to sow the seeds of love unto the Lord and others, and in the next season see a harvest in, through, and to your life.

Grace be unto you, and peace, from God our Father, and from the Lord Jesus Christ. (Philippians 1:2)

PART 37

Your Journey

And the Lord answered me, and said, "Write the vision, and make it plain upon tables, that he may run that readeth it. (Habakkuk 2:2)

Where there is no vision, the people perish: but he that keepeth the law, happy is he. (Proverbs 29:18)

And it shall come to pass in the last days, saith God, I will pour out of My Spirit upon all flesh: and your sons and your daughters shall prophesy, and your young men shall see visions, and your old men shall dream dreams. (Acts 2:17)

Make a journal. Writing your visions and dreams from the Lord is important. A journal stores the memories in your subconscious for recall by the Holy Spirit as needed.
Ask yourself these questions:

- *What are my revelations, visions, and dreams from the Lord?*
- *What does scripture say to me, in my own words?*
- *How will I apply these passages?*

PART 38

Your Kingdom Keys

Thankfulness

> Enter into His Gates with thanksgiving, and into His courts with praise: be thankful unto Him, and bless His name. (Psalm 100:4)

> In everything give thanks: for this is the will of God in Christ Jesus concerning you. (1 Thessalonians 5:18)

> Giving thanks always for all things unto God and the Father in the name of our Lord Jesus Christ. (Ephesians 5:20)

> Be careful for nothing; but in everything by prayer and supplication with thanksgiving let your request be made unto God. And the peace of God, which passeth all understanding, shall keep your hearts and minds through Christ Jesus. (Philippians 4:6–7)

As long as we have breath, we can find something to be thankful about.

Praise

I will bless the Lord at all times: His praise shall continually be in my mouth. (Psalm 34:1)

Let my mouth be filled with Thy praise and with Thy honor all the day. (Psalm 71:8)

Whoso offereth praise glorifieth Me: and to him that ordereth his conversation aright will I show the salvation of God. (Psalm 50:23)

But Thou art holy, O Thou that inhabitest the praises of Israel. (Psalm 22:3)

Great is the Lord, and greatly to be praised; and His greatness is unsearchable. (Psalm 145:3)

The Lord will be in you and with you.

Worship

Give unto the Lord the glory due His name: bring an offering, and come before Him: worship the Lord in the beauty of His Holiness. (1 Chronicles 16:29)

But the hour cometh, and now is when the true worshippers shall worship the Father in spirit and truth: for the Father seeketh such to worship Him. (John 4:23)

Just imagine being sought by the Lord!

APPENDIX

Questions for You and as a Group Minister to Encourage Discussion with Attendees

This material is designed to promote further thought and discussion about each topic, and to encourage participants to share personal experiences and testimonies.

Whosoever will be great among you, let him be your minister.
(Matthew 20:26)

What does this message say to you?
How can this message be applicable in your life?
How must you change?
What steps are you taking to apply these truths to your life?
Who are you going to share this message with before we meet again?

★★★

Let's discuss what we have learned today:

What are you thankful for this week?
What has worried you this week?
What do you need to make the situation better?
What are the needs of the people in your sphere of influence?
How can we help one another with the needs we have expressed?

★★★

The Lord bless thee, and keep thee:
The Lord make His face to shine upon
thee, and be gracious unto thee:
The Lord lift up His countenance
upon thee, and give thee peace.
—Numbers 6:24–26

Printed in the United States
by Baker & Taylor Publisher Services